JUNIOR BIOGRAPHIES

D1245979

DRAKE
ACTOR AND RAPPER

Enslow Publishing
101 W. 23rd Street
Suite 240
New York, NY 10011
USA

enslow.com

Hannah Isbell

agent A person who helps actors, musicians, or other artists to find work and become well-known.

album A collection of songs on a single CD or record.

collaborating Working together.

income Money received from work.

melody A group of musical notes that can be put together to make a song.

mixtape A collection of songs that is not released through a record label.

single A song released on its own.

tracks The songs on an album.

variety A group of different things.

CONTENTS

Drake

CHAPTER 1

STARTING FROM THE BOTTOM

In 2016, Drake released his sixth number one album in a row, *Views*. The album broke records, topped the charts, and sold over a million copies in its first week! There is no doubt that Drake is a star.

A Canadian rapper, singer, and songwriter, Drake, who is sometimes called "Drizzy," is known for his unique blend of rap and melody. His mixture of musical styles has made his music popular with rap fans, R&B fans, and pop music fans all over the world. He has earned many awards and is one of the most successful music stars in the world. Drake describes his own rise to fame in the lyrics, "Started from the bottom, now we here."

Drake and his mom, Sandi Graham, on the red carpet in 2011

MUSIC IN HIS BLOOD

Drake's full name is Aubrey Drake Graham. He was born in Toronto, Ontario, Canada, on October 24, 1986. His father, Dennis Graham, is an African American musician from Memphis, Tennessee. Two of his uncles are also musicians, and Drake grew up listening to many different kinds of music. This **variety** would inspire his style in the future.

According to Drake, though, his biggest influence while growing up was his mother, Sandi Graham, a Jewish Canadian teacher.

RAISED BY A SINGLE MOM

Drake's parents divorced when he was just five years old. He stayed with his mother in Toronto when his father moved back to Memphis. Sometimes Drake would visit his father in the summer, but mostly his mother raised him as a single parent.

Views was Drake's fourth studio album. His first three were *Thank Me Later* (2010), *Take Care* (2011), and *Nothing Was the Same* (2013).

His family struggled with money at first. They lived in a poor neighborhood in Toronto, and times were often hard for them. But mother and son relied on each other to get through those tough times. Now Drake sings and raps about his mother on many of his tracks, including the lyrics, "It's our world, it's just us two."

Drake Says:

"I don't want to get too emotional, but I had to hug her. My father doesn't stay with us, so I had to be security for her and just let her know that everything is going to be all right."

Long before Drake started rapping and singing on stage, he could be seen on TV screens across Canada as a young actor.

Drake and his mother moved into a small house they shared with another family. This house was in a much wealthier neighborhood, and Drake was sent to a new school. He was sometimes bullied at school for being different. The fact that he was poor, mixed race, and Jewish made him stand out to bullies. His new school did give him a great opportunity, though—it is where he started acting!

BECOMING A STAR

Drake began performing when he was fifteen years old. He started acting in high school drama classes. The

Drake went to high school at Forest Hill Collegiate Institute.

father of one of Drake's friends was an **agent**, and he liked Drake's acting. After doing a few commercials, Drake got a role playing a disabled basketball player on the Canadian teen drama *Degrassi: The Next Generation.*

Degrassi: The Next Generation was a popular show in both Canada and the United States. The show followed the lives of teenage characters dealing with important issues like bullying and self-image. It won many awards.

Drake starred in the show from 2001 until 2007. During some of that time, his acting work provided the only income the family had.

Sadly, Drake dropped out of school. The bullying, his acting work, and his family's struggles had made things very hard for him. Later, he found the strength to go back to his studies and earn a GED, which is a test that shows that a person has a high school education.

Drake Says:

"My mother was very sick. We were very poor, like broke. The only money I had coming in was off of Canadian TV."

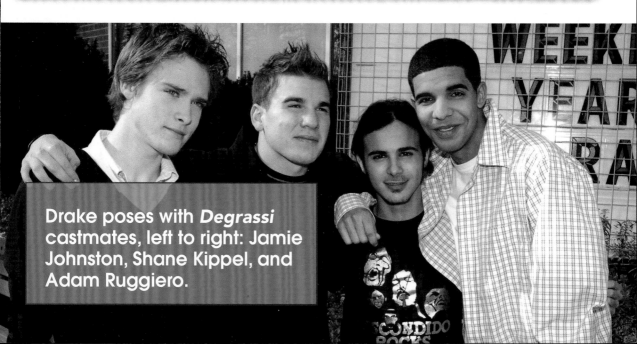

Drake poses with *Degrassi* castmates, left to right: Jamie Johnston, Shane Kippel, and Adam Ruggiero.

CHAPTER 3
MOVING ON TO MUSIC

Drake was not only interested in acting. He was inspired by musicians like Jay Z, Kanye West, and Aaliyah. He decided to start creating his own music. He released his first **mixtape**, *Room for Improvement,* on his own and sold over six thousand copies. His second mixtape, *Comeback Season,* was what really started his career in music, though.

The mixtape included the **single** "Replacement Girl," and the song became very popular. It caught the attention

Drake Says:

"Live without pretending, Love without depending, Listen without defending, Speak without offending."

Lil Wayne and Drake perform at the 2009 BET Awards.

Drake performs with Jay Z at Yankee Stadium in 2010.

of hip-hop star Lil Wayne. He invited Drake to perform with him. The two artists recorded many songs together.

It became clear that the differences that made him a target of bullying in school were now strengths. His music was unique, and many people started to notice.

BREAKTHROUGH

Drake's next mixtape, *So Far Gone,* was even more successful than the one before. Soon, Drake's music could be heard on the radio across Canada and the United States, and people were downloading his music every day! His songs started to appear on music charts, and in 2010, he won the Juno Awards Rap Recording of the Year.

Drake would go on to collaborate on music with many of the artists who first inspired him, including Jay Z and Kanye West.

Drake wins big at the 2010 Juno Awards.

The Juno Award was just the first of many awards for Drake. In 2010, he released his first album, *Thank Me Later*. It reached the number one spot on the charts on its first day! Drake's career was taking off like a rocket.

Critics praised Drake's voice as well as his lyrics, which are often very personal. People also loved the way he could easily move between musical styles. Drake's popularity kept growing and he kept on releasing more singles and albums. He worked to keep his style fresh and collaborate

Drake has won over twenty awards for his music, music videos, and acting! Among his many awards was the NAACP (National Associatioin for the Advancement of Colored People) Image Award, which he shared with Mary J. Blige in 2012.

Drake in concert in New Orleans, 2010

with other artists. He also looked to Middle Eastern and Caribbean music for more inspiration.

BRANCHING OUT

Drake has also kept up with his acting, starring as a voice actor in the movie *Ice Age 2: Continental Drift,* and appearing on TV as a special guest. He has done all this while continuing to make new music and even starting his own record production company!

Drake attends a basketball game between the LA Lakers and the Golden State Warriors in November 2016.

Drake accepts his award at the 2016 American Music Awards.

Drake Says:

"It was my father who told me there is no rapper who is singing and rapping. He told me that in order to be successful you're going to have to do something different than what everyone else is doing."

In 2013, Drake won a Grammy, one of the highest music awards. He won for Best Rap Album of the Year. By 2016, he had won two MTV Music Video Awards and been nominated for Grammy Awards twenty-seven times! With the help of friends, the support of his family, and through his own hard work, Drake truly started at the bottom and rose to the top. The key to his success? He was never afraid to be different and stand out from the crowd!

TIMELINE

1986 Aubrey Drake Graham is born in Toronto, Ontario, Canada, on October 24.

2001 Drake stars as Jimmy Brooks on *Degrassi: The Next Generation*.

2006 Releases his first mixtape, *Room for Improvement*.

2009 "Replacement Girl" is aired on TV, bringing Drake a new audience.

2010 Drake wins the Juno Award for Rap Recording of the Year.

2013 Becomes "Global Ambassador" for the Toronto Raptors.

2013 Wins the Grammy for Best Rap Album.

2016 *Views* is released.

BOOKS

Cornish, Melanie J. *The History of Hip Hop*. New York, NY: Crabtree Publishing, 2009.

Foley, Cindy. *I Am Hip Hop*. Orlando, FL: Child of This Culture, 2013.

Giovanni, Nikki. *Hip Hop Speaks to Children*. Naperville, IL: Sourcebooks Inc., 2008.

WEBSITES

Drake's Fansite
www.drizzydrake.org
Drake's fansite where you can find discussions, photos, and talk about Drake.

Drake Official
www.drakeofficial.com
Drake's official website where you can find song lyrics, tour dates, photos, and news.

INDEX

Published in 2018 by Enslow Publishing, LLC.
101 W. 23rd Street, Suite 240, New York, NY 10011

Library of Congress Cataloging-in-Publication Data
Names: Isbell, Hannah, author.
Title: Drake : actor and rapper / Hannah Isbell.
Description: New York : Enslow Publishing, 2018. | Series: Junior biographies | Includes bibliographical references and index. | Audience: Grades 3-5.
Identifiers: LCCN 2017003123| ISBN 9780766086685 (library-bound) | ISBN 9780766087897 (pbk.) | ISBN 9780766087903 (6-pack)
Subjects: LCSH: Drake, 1986—Juvenile literature. | Rap musicians–Canada–Biography–Juvenile literature. | Actors–Canada–Biography–Juvenile literature.
Classification: LCC ML3930.D73 I83 2017 | DDC 782.421649092 [B] –dc23
LC record available at https://lccn.loc.gov/2017003123

Printed in the United States of America

Photo Credits: Cover, p. 1 Gabe Ginsberg/Getty Images; p. 4 © Owen Sweeney/Invision/AP; pp. 6, 11, 16 George Pimentel/WireImage/Getty Images; p. 10 SimonP/Wikimedia; p. 13 John Shearer/WireImage/Getty Images; p. 14 Kevin Mazur/WireImage/Getty Images; p. 18 Scott Legato/FilmMagic/Getty Images; p. 19 Noel Vasquez/GC Images/Getty Images; p. 20 Michael Tran/FilmMagic/Getty Images; back cover, pp. 2, 3, 22, 23, 24 (curves graphic) Alena Kazlouskaya/Shutterstock.com; interior pages (crowd) solarseven/Shutterstock.com.